Saturn

Anna Mohanty

BookLeaf Publishing

India | USA | UK

Presentation by *BookLeaf Publishing*

Web: www.bookleafpub.com

E-mail: info@bookleafpub.com

ISBN: 9789363310674

First edition 2024

ACKNOWLEDGEMENT

I have endless gratitude for the healthcare professionals I have watched in my own medical journey, personally and academically. I want this book to be a tribute to cosmic levels of bravery by healthcare providers and patients everyday. Thank you to the patients whose stories I am privileged to tell.

Quickly Before The Moon Rises

Saturn rings church bells
As the bullet hole in my mother's stomach
Is stitched by piano strings and hidden in the
keys of a pearl necklace
That unlock an apartment that sees meteors
brimming over the capitol
The fire escape hidden in red-white-and-blue
ribbons
Because a ship docked at Venus's shore without
leaving footprints
Or if they were there, they were swallowed by
the tide
Like her glasses the day in Cape Canaveral
She dove into catch the tether I clung to
As the ball of the pendulum
Ticking seconds after the undertow pulled me
down like gravity warping time
Did she ever wonder why I bobbed to the
surface like a cork
Popping from a champagne bottle? Like the
elastic sound
Of ospreys hiding the surface of a wave
Spilling salt water turned taffy in jet fuel over
the tide before the moon rises

And Saturn stepping after to fill vacant
fluorescent lights in waiting rooms
That begin to smell like summer

Diagnosed with osteoporosis onset by
osteosarcoma

Nana Catches a Cold Swimming in the River

Blue-green Atlantic
Nana's communion dress billowing to keep her
afloat
The bubble of the Arctic on a topography globe
The Arctic sea around her, white on the bottom
A penguin camouflaging the ice as to not be
taken by sharks
Her father leaned back on the dock to take a
smoke break
Always cigars, never cigarettes
To match his daughter: the cork in the English
Channel

Gloss magazine swimsuit models pinned on the
icebox
Gleaned from the glint of the fluorescent bulbs:
like angels
Keep the fridge door shut and we can always see
them

The Night of her funeral:
My bony heels clicking on kitchen linoleum
Nana's kitchen smells like the plastic lids on
unopened milk cartons

You can pour it like whiskey into Waterford
crystal glasses
And I dunk Oreos in it
Holding them in my forefingers like a cigarette

Diagnosed post-mortem with hydrophobia

Kitchen Garden

The floors are wonderfully linoleum
Mildew blossoming in like sidewalk cracks
Venous plumbing sags
Sputtering in myocardial infarction
Fostering a spider family
Who will holiday at the bend towards the washer
Dish towels pregnant with lichen
Pale in the light of a stained glass butterfly
That draws honeybees in pilgrimage
To the windowsill shrine of the former tsar
Royal weddings, births of heirs framed in plaster
Now springs the aster from jars
In the wake of the apex predator
His brick oxygen tank at the cul-de-sac peak
Will outlive him

Diagnosed with double cataracts and moved to
assisted living

The Left-Handed Author

The novel came in with scoliosis in its spine
Her back ringing in church bells
The arthritis in her left hand is jotted down in
her chart
As a fabric cover embroidered by an gloved
hand
The thimble denting the small flap of skin where
Her fingers join in what's left of prayer
And valleys run between her metatarsals
Cradling blue vein rivers
Which we thought as children had no oxygen
But we see now under a microscope harboring
an endangered ecosystem
That inhales anaerobically in a violet sunset on a
horizon
Where a forest of papyrus trees has burned for
72 years
Sputtering black dots of ashen ink that clings to
its trunks like lichen
Revealing an ischemic blue sky speckled with
white dots
Constellations of words she's forgotten

Diagnosed post-stroke with Alien Hand
Syndrome

Off I-95

She made her body a gas station
For post-divorce or pre-divorce/post-love
Pontiacs to drink diesel
And complain about their wives
A seedy don't-sit-on-the-toilet-seat,
bring-your-own-glass kind of palace
Men were served microwave apple pie on paper
plates
And asked for alamode
Because they would gorge themselves at a
roadside dinner
And fall asleep fast from molasses-dipped
melatonin
Undressed from the top up in motel sheets
Where she left them dreaming of satisfaction

In a fatal misinterpretation of a neon Open 24/7
sign in the window she was
Misdiagnosed with neurosyphilis

Heart Rhythm

And tell her newborn daughter that when they
tried to stitch the incision
A rebellion broke out across the arced canyon
into her uterus
As if the stream of blood was damned to be
dammed
Until someone looked inside her at 27
The grandmother said as a child growing up in
New Haven she was a doll
Medical history saying she was born limp in the
Yale hospital as burlap
Until her muscles were tuned at eight by a cello
teacher
Who played pizzicato down her spine like she
was another instrument
The Yale Daily News reviewed of his first
composition:
"In key, but out of touch. Cursed to play music,
never to create it"
And he shredded the sheet music for his solo
symphony he had written on linen napkins
At his parents' anniversary dinner
Moved to music by the crystal chandelier and
triumphant champagne he thought was love
In the ambulance her skin cut like cloth

Diagnosed with postpartum depression

9

Mirror Meadow

The tipping point of entropy is when telomeres
unravel like spools of thread
And she herself blossoms like April dandelions
across her chest
Half-balded seeds metastasizing almost invisibly
On a backdrop of linen white sheets tied to a
clothes line
Left to dry after her sponge bath
Each new flower that lights like fireflies on an
ultrasound
Is a self-portrait drawn with a puddle as a mirror
Obscured by oak leaf lily pads roots are
sketched
From the worst memory of ourselves

Diagnosed with breast cancer requiring a double
mastectomy

Harbor Lullaby

Breakwaves break sea glass
Cast sunfast
Magenta Aurora borealis
Glazing alabaster albatross
Native to my neck
In a fleck
Of campfire sunlight
That turns plastic into
Diamonds choking gulls
Drinking the silver sea
And falling into ebony
At the point cargo ships sail off the Earth
In honor of the menagerie
Where sailboats will be tipped by the spin of a
fan
And skulls are cracked by masts
His neck cradled at shore by a sandpiper's
wingspan

He and the hull of his boat are
Diagnosed with a spinal fracture

Linoleum

Scarlett blossoms under a safety pinned sari
And her mother gives her turmeric to ease the
tightening
Of her belly as her blood drips onto pink
linoleum
Bumble bees hum through an open window
Smelling a bud as it swells
And is cut for the kitchen vase
Magenta tinged brown at the edges
Before she is taken to the honey
She must walk through the spice market
Leaving a trail of bright red petals in her wake
Like male cardinals dropping feathers like coins
at her feet
Languishing in bones born hollow enough to fly

Diagnosed with menopause-related osteoporosis

Emergency Department on New Year's Eve

It is the Year of the Chrysalis
And I don't know why she's draped in white
With wax wings melting like butter pats
Alcohol rotting in her lungs after
She collapsed at the Baltimore pier in
mid-December
Overwhelmed by the height of the ferris wheel
As she kept her face pressed against the glass
Looking magpie-like for fish glinting in the
water
Which she will feast on in septets if she is
allowed home for Christmas
While starlight dewdrops on the motor that
maintains her cyclical flight
At midnight it is the Year of the Butterfly
And she is lost in the eclipse's Path of Totality
Chasing monarchs chasing milkweed
In a nomad van with a seafoam green stripe
That bands the engine burning boiling-over pots
And cool air icing the moon in the rearview
And she will be gone before Halley's Comet
returns

Undiagnosed, the patient left without consult

Orbital

Atrophic scars from heroin healed over to look
like spider veins chain her left arm
She had kept the right for tennis and let the left
one heal to cradle her son
Against her chest as red spots begin to mark his
back like a map of state capitals
Tracking mountain ranges across his back in
purple rings
Like a shadow of his mother's forearm makes
his spinal cord where she holds him
From fear that any needles will touch him
Not that they will lace his blood with mercury
like they say
But that he will be pulled into the orbit of her
star and
Become Mercury:
At the closest ring to burn with here until she
swallows him
In the corner a Spider Man night light faintly
glows
And casts shadows of monitors stretched like a
funhouse mirror across the ceiling
And he laughs that they look like rabbits
popping from magic hats

Diagnosed with measles and pneumonia

The Voyager

She can only afford standing room on a plane
To be launched the same day as the astronauts
Across an ocean as the wings bend backward
Like the shape of a flock of geese
Eating crumbs of naan as her husband reads a
magazine
On how America now reaches the moon
And Ford engines reach 114,000 miles
Home and back 284 times if America would
build across
Instead of upwards
Where her husband looks
To see snow burying their car port like piles of
gold
Not realizing the flecks of yellow are not ore but
dog piss
And she smiles faintly at his wonder as
Her bare feet swell on Maryland winter
pavement
She walks to the bus station outside the family
court
Snapping a marriage like raw sugar cane to suck
the marrow:
She has died twice once
And she will die a second

From pneumonia that finds her feeding puffed
wedding rice
To a nest of birds that forgot to migrate

Diagnosed with hypothermia

Passive Voice

Verbal propositions were used
To move her queen into checkmate across
stained carbon wood kitchen tiles
That sagged in August humidity
Later patient expressed no fear as knife drawer
was positioned behind her
Cast iron skillet hanging behind him was
forgotten
That and he was raised by a father who flipped
over chess boards when games were lost
There was an imaginary line drawn between the
end of her index finger
And his temple
Another parallax line was drawn between her
two lips and her tulip bridal bouquet
Which led to the creation of the illusion of depth
in her argument
When her eyelids were shuttered in violet
Her face was flattened to a window pane
And an imprint like laid brick was left in her
skin by boot marks
She resembled a house not built to withstand a
hurricane

Diagnosed with a basilar skull fracture

Campfire Story

At only eleven years old the electrical
engineering prodigy
Invented a self-lighting bong with a freshly
emptied beer bottle
And fridge magnets attached to fishing wire
To create eddy currents to cyclotronically stir
electrons
While his mother cycled the garden hose around
the tobacco barn
Which burned when a weed-induced epiphany
of how is
Electron magnetic moment is a constant value
Knocked over the bottled fire
Sending the Manassas barn and the leaves in
side
Into biblical pillars of fire
Which the local farmers gathered around to roast
s'mores
With marshmallow cores labeled a controlled
substance by the state of Virginia
He wrote the end of the story in chalk on the
board next to the quantum Hall effect equation
When he was tired of coughing it out

Diagnosed with paraseptal emphysema

The Interview

Do you have a moment apart from snare drums?
Your greatest fear having become the people
Who think you're scared of them
That they sound like gunfire when you insist a
marching tune
As if you marched and March
Was not the month of cigarettes and solitaire
As monsoon season became a tide for shotgun
shells
In the year of the Swamp Creatures with backs
draped in moss
The year everyone was sent to the moon or to
Asia
When each were equally foreign
If you remember anything
Now is the time to write it down
Because paper is the only thing that will survive
this
And all you recall is the cardstock breakfast
menu

Diagnosed with post-traumatic amnesia

The Steel King

Chromium beams arch over the ghost of a
railway
That reflects the tide of the moon
In the water that reflects its defiance
To exit the night sky like a pellet in doe hide
Rather revolve through the month in ebbing
levels of gloom
This is his wishing well
With slats between train tracks just like arcade
coin slots
When the net was removed after construction
The one used to catch falling rebar and the
throats of gulls
His greatest achievement was not thinking of a
flight
In which even if the gravity well mistakenly
took him as a payment
The Potomac would catch him
From a fall only a a few meters taller than an
Olympic dive
To reward his good behavior
He spent the loose quarters to buy a cigarette
That he held to close to the gas tank of a cab he
hired

To drive the 0.1 miles across the bridge so he
could watch the landscape of his kingdom
From a mustard yellow carriage

Diagnosed with second degree burns of the torso

Night Job

At 4am the vinyl drags him through the bluest
blues
And as he spins to the dissonant crackles of
scratched needles
And the metal cylinder of his music box's hitting
notes on a finger harp
He balances himself in the three-body problem
as their gravity's coiled
Between masculinity and femininity
Asteroid belts of Mardi Gras beads entangling in
a cocktail dress
That cuts rolls of fat at his shoulders leaving an
indent against his collarbone like a corset
The strict posture of womanhood is enticing to a
man whose mind works in stock market ticks
He fixed a cherry chapstick to his upper lip
Hoping the heat will make the color run as if his
lips and chin were rouged by a cherry pie
He will say his wife baked for him when he goes
to the office in four hours
The nocturnal wife who leaves him a tray of
biscuits and gravy each morning
Growing both their bellies

Diagnosed with acute cardiovascular syndrome
brought on by sleep deprivation

In Hunt

A flash like helium fission in the core of an
asterisk
Glints across her eye
Like a colt's shadow slightly darker than her
pupils
In the forest of her mind she harbors a colony of
footnotes
That hum hymns of reservation
And read from the book by her bedside
Bloating a binary typed in black and white
But where their flames flicker in multicolored
fireworks
When its pages reach fahrenheit 451
As cities are burnt and resurrected in nothing
more than a prayer candle
With watercolor roses autographed with a
toothpick
Which she lights with a gas station matchbook
To spook the runaway foal to flee from its own
shadow silhouetted against the plastic curtain
It will carve its hooves like honeycomb on
brambles
Till it pauses to watch the surface tension
breaking a pool of gray matter
In a dark matter downpour

Diagnosed with lactic acidosis after refused
blood transfusion

www.ingramcontent.com/pod-product-compliance
Lightning Source LLC
LaVergne TN
LVHW050504210726
843509LV00015BA/2991